CONTENTS

CHEESECAKE PARTY POPS... **4**

BROWN SUGAR CHEESECAKE
WITH BOURBON SAUCE **6**

NEW YORK CHEESECAKE... **8**

BAVARIAN APPLE TORTE **10**

CHOCOLATE-VANILLA SWIRL CHEESECAKE.......... **12**

CHOCOLATE-RASPBERRY THUMBPRINTS **14**

CHOCOLATE TURTLE CHEESECAKE **16**

NEW YORK-STYLE STRAWBERRY-SWIRL
CHEESECAKE SQUARES... **18**

LEMON-CREAM CHEESE CUPCAKES **20**

CHOCOLATE ELEGANCE.. **22**

SIMPLY SENSATIONAL TRUFFLES **24**

CREAMY LEMON NUT BARS **26**

TIRAMISU BOWL **28**

RED VELVET CUPCAKES **30**

CHEESECAKE PARTY POPS

PREP: 30 min. \ **TOTAL:** 10 hours 45 min. \ **MAKES:** 42 servings

---

3 pkg. (8 oz. each) *Philadelphia* Cream Cheese, softened

¾ cup sugar

1 tsp. vanilla

2 eggs

8 oz. *Baker's* White Chocolate

8 oz. *Baker's* Semi-Sweet Chocolate

1 **Heat** oven to 325°F.

2 **Line** 13×9-inch pan with foil, with ends of foil extending over sides. Beat cream cheese, sugar and vanilla with mixer until well blended. Add eggs, 1 at a time, mixing after each just until blended. Pour into prepared pan.

3 **Bake** 35 min. or until center is set. Cool completely. Refrigerate 4 hours.

4 **Use** foil handles to lift cheesecake from pan before cutting into 42 squares. Roll each square into ball; place on parchment paper-covered baking sheet. Insert 1 lollipop stick into center of each. Freeze 4 hours.

5 **Melt** chocolates in separate bowls as directed on packages. Dip 21 lollipops in white chocolate; return to baking sheet. Repeat with remaining lollipops and semi-sweet chocolate. Drizzle remaining melted chocolate of contrasting color over lollipops. Refrigerate 1 hour or until chocolate is firm.

BROWN SUGAR CHEESECAKE WITH BOURBON SAUCE

PREP: 20 min. \ **TOTAL:** 6 hours 5 min. \ **MAKES:** 12 servings

---

- ¾ cup butter, divided
- 15 chocolate sandwich cookies, finely crushed (about 1¼ cups)
- 3 pkg. (8 oz. each) *Philadelphia* Cream Cheese, softened
- 1¾ cups packed brown sugar, divided
- 1 Tbsp. vanilla
- 3 eggs
- ½ cup whipping cream
- ¼ cup bourbon

1 **Heat** oven to 350°F.

2 **Melt** ¼ cup butter; mix with cookie crumbs until well blended. Press onto bottom of 9-inch springform pan.

3 **Beat** cream cheese, ¾ cup sugar and vanilla in large bowl with mixer until well blended. Add eggs, 1 at a time, beating on low speed after each just until blended. Pour over crust.

4 **Bake** 40 to 45 min. or until center is almost set. Run knife around rim of pan to loosen cake; cool completely before removing rim. Refrigerate 4 hours.

5 **Meanwhile,** bring cream, bourbon, remaining butter and sugar to boil in saucepan; simmer on medium-low heat 7 to 10 min. or until slightly thickened, stirring constantly. Cool. Refrigerate until ready to serve.

6 **Pour** bourbon sauce into microwaveable bowl. Microwave on HIGH 30 sec. or just until warmed; stir. Spoon 2 Tbsp. over each serving of cheesecake just before serving.

NON-ALCOHOLIC VARIATION
Substitute 2 tsp. vanilla for the bourbon.

NEW YORK CHEESECAKE

PREP: 15 min. \ **TOTAL:** 5 hours 35 min. \ **MAKES:** 16 servings

---

1 **cup graham cracker crumbs**

3 **Tbsp. sugar**

3 **Tbsp. butter, melted**

5 **pkg. (8 oz. each)** *Philadelphia* **Cream Cheese, softened**

1 **cup sugar**

3 **Tbsp. flour**

1 **Tbsp. vanilla**

1 **cup** *Breakstone's* **or** *Knudsen* **Sour Cream**

4 **eggs**

1 **can (21 oz.) cherry pie filling**

1 **Heat** oven to 325°F.

2 **Mix** graham crumbs, 3 Tbsp. sugar and butter; press onto bottom of 9-inch springform pan. Bake 10 min.

3 **Beat** cream cheese, 1 cup sugar, flour and vanilla in large bowl with electric mixer on medium speed until well blended. Add sour cream; mix well. Add eggs, 1 at a time, mixing on low speed after each addition just until blended. Pour over crust.

4 **Bake** 1 hour 10 min. or until center is almost set. Run knife or metal spatula around rim of pan to loosen cake; cool before removing rim of pan. Refrigerate 4 hours. Top with pie filling before serving.

SPECIAL EXTRA

Omit cherry pie filling. Prepare and refrigerate cheesecake as directed. Top with 2 cups mixed berries. Brush with 2 Tbsp. strawberry jelly, melted.

NOTE

If using a dark nonstick 9-inch springform pan, reduce oven temperature to 300°F.

BAVARIAN APPLE TORTE

PREP: 30 min. \ **TOTAL:** 4 hours 5 min. \ **MAKES:** 12 servings

---

- ½ cup butter, softened
- 1 cup sugar, divided
- 1 cup flour
- 1 pkg. (8 oz.) *Philadelphia* Cream Cheese, softened
- 1 egg
- ½ tsp. vanilla
- ½ tsp. ground cinnamon
- 4 Granny Smith or Golden Delicious apples, peeled, sliced
- ¼ cup *Planters* Sliced Almonds

1 Heat oven to 425°F.

2 Beat butter and ⅓ cup sugar in small bowl with electric mixer on medium speed until light and fluffy. Add flour; mix well. Spread onto bottom and 1 inch up side of 9-inch springform pan.

3 Beat cream cheese and ⅓ cup of the remaining sugar in same bowl with electric mixer on medium speed until well blended. Add egg and vanilla; mix well. Spread evenly over crust. Combine remaining ⅓ cup sugar and cinnamon. Add to apples in large bowl; toss to coat. Spoon over cream cheese layer; sprinkle with almonds.

4 Bake 10 min. Reduce temperature to 375°F; continue baking 25 min. or until center is set. Cool on wire rack. Loosen torte from rim of pan. Refrigerate 3 hours.

SUBSTITUTE

Substitute chopped *Planters* Pecans for the sliced almonds.

CHOCOLATE-VANILLA SWIRL CHEESECAKE

PREP: 15 min. \ **TOTAL:** 5 hours 25 min. \ **MAKES:** 16 servings

- 20 **chocolate sandwich cookies, finely crushed (about 2 cups)**
- 3 **Tbsp. butter, melted**
- 4 **pkg. (8 oz. each)** *Philadelphia* **Cream Cheese, softened**
- 1 **cup sugar**
- 1 **tsp. vanilla**
- 1 **cup** *Breakstone's* **or** *Knudsen* **Sour Cream**
- 4 **eggs**
- 6 **oz.** *Baker's* **Semi-Sweet Chocolate, melted, cooled**

1 **Heat** oven to 325°F.

2 **Mix** cookie crumbs and butter; press onto bottom of foil-lined 13×9-inch pan. Bake 10 min.

3 **Beat** cream cheese, sugar and vanilla in large bowl with mixer until well blended. Add sour cream; mix well. Add eggs, 1 at a time, mixing after each just until blended.

4 **Reserve** 1 cup batter. Stir chocolate into remaining batter; pour over crust. Top with spoonfuls of reserved batter.

5 **Swirl** batters with knife. Bake 40 min. or until center is almost set. Cool. Refrigerate 4 hours.

SPECIAL EXTRA

Garnish with chocolate curls just before serving. Use a vegetable peeler to shave the side of an additional 1 oz. *Baker's* Semi-Sweet Chocolate until desired amount of curls is obtained. Wrap remaining chocolate and store at room temperature for another use.

CHOCOLATE-RASPBERRY THUMBPRINTS

PREP: 20 min. \ **TOTAL:** 45 min. \ **MAKES:** 4½ doz. or 27 servings, 2 cookies each

---

- 2 **cups flour**
- 1 **tsp. baking soda**
- ¼ **tsp. salt**
- 4 **oz. *Baker's* Unsweetened Chocolate**
- ½ **cup butter**
- 1 **pkg. (8 oz.) *Philadelphia* Cream Cheese, cubed, softened**
- 1¼ **cups sugar, divided**
- 1 **egg**
- 1 **tsp. vanilla**
- ⅓ **cup strawberry jam**

1 **Mix** flour, baking soda and salt. Microwave chocolate and butter in large microwaveable bowl on HIGH 2 min.; stir until chocolate is completely melted. Add cream cheese; stir until blended. Stir in 1 cup sugar, egg and vanilla. Add flour; mix well. Refrigerate 15 min.

2 **Heat** oven to 375°F. Roll dough into 1-inch balls; coat with remaining sugar. Place, 2 inches apart, on baking sheets. Press your thumb into center of each ball; fill each indentation with about ¼ tsp. jam.

3 **Bake** 8 to 10 min. or until lightly browned. Cool 1 min. on baking sheets; transfer to wire racks. Cool completely.

SUBSTITUTE
Prepare using your favorite flavor of jam.

CHOCOLATE TURTLE CHEESECAKE

PREP: 15 min. \ **TOTAL:** 5 hours 50 min. \ **MAKES:** 16 servings

---

1½ **cups crushed vanilla wafers (about 50)**

¾ **cup chopped *Planters* Pecans, divided**

¼ **cup butter, melted**

32 ***Kraft* Caramels**

3 **Tbsp. milk**

4 **pkg. (8 oz. each) *Philadelphia* Cream Cheese, softened**

1 **cup sugar**

1 **cup *Breakstone's* or *Knudsen* Sour Cream**

4 **eggs**

8 **oz. *Baker's* Semi-Sweet Chocolate, divided**

1 **Heat** oven to 325°F.

2 **Mix** wafer crumbs, ½ cup nuts and butter; press onto bottom of 13✕9-inch pan. Microwave caramels and milk in microwaveable bowl on MEDIUM (50%) 4 to 5 min. or until caramels are melted and mixture is well blended, stirring every 2 min. Pour over crust; spread to within 1 inch of edge. Cool.

3 **Beat** cream cheese and sugar with mixer until blended. Add sour cream; mix well. Add eggs, 1 at a time, mixing on low speed after each just until blended. Melt 7 oz. chocolate. Stir into cream cheese batter; pour over caramel layer.

4 **Bake** 45 to 50 min. or until center is almost set. Cool completely. Refrigerate 4 hours. Sprinkle with remaining nuts just before serving. Melt remaining chocolate; drizzle over cheesecake.

COOKING KNOW-HOW

For easy slicing, run a knife under hot water to warm up, then wipe dry before using to cut cheesecake. For best results, clean the knife after each slice.

NEW YORK-STYLE STRAWBERRY-SWIRL CHEESECAKE SQUARES

PREP: 20 min. \ **TOTAL:** 6 hours \ **MAKES:** 16 servings

- **1 cup graham cracker crumbs**
- **3 Tbsp. sugar**
- **3 Tbsp. butter, melted**
- **5 pkg. (8 oz. each)** *Philadelphia* **Cream Cheese, softened**
- **1 cup sugar**
- **3 Tbsp. flour**
- **1 Tbsp. vanilla**
- **1 cup** *Breakstone's* **or** *Knudsen* **Sour Cream**
- **4 eggs**
- **⅓ cup seedless strawberry jam**

1 Heat oven to 325°F.

2 Line 13×9-inch pan with foil, with ends of foil extending over sides. Mix graham crumbs, 3 Tbsp. sugar and butter; press onto bottom of pan. Bake 10 min.

3 Beat cream cheese, 1 cup sugar, flour and vanilla with mixer until well blended. Add sour cream; mix well. Add eggs, 1 at a time, mixing on low speed after each just until blended. Pour over crust. Drop small spoonfuls of jam over batter; swirl gently with knife.

4 Bake 40 min. or until center is almost set. Cool completely. Refrigerate 4 hours. Use foil handles to remove cheesecake from pan before cutting to serve.

LEMON-CREAM CHEESE CUPCAKES

PREP: 15 min. \ **TOTAL:** 1 hour 39 min. \ **MAKES:** 24 servings

---

- **1 pkg. (2-layer size) white cake mix**
- **1 pkg. (3.4 oz.) *Jell-O* Lemon Flavor Instant Pudding**
- **1 cup water**
- **4 egg whites**
- **2 Tbsp. oil**
- **1 pkg. (8 oz.) *Philadelphia* Cream Cheese, softened**
- **¼ cup butter, softened**
- **2 Tbsp. lemon juice**
- **1 pkg. (16 oz.) powdered sugar**

1 Heat oven to 350°F.

2 Beat first 5 ingredients in large bowl with mixer on low speed 1 min. or until dry ingredients are moistened. (Batter will be thick.) Beat on medium speed 2 min. Spoon into 24 paper-lined muffin cups.

3 Bake 21 to 24 min. or until toothpick inserted in centers comes out clean. Cool in pans 10 min.; remove to wire racks. Cool completely.

4 Beat cream cheese, butter and lemon juice in large bowl with mixer until well blended. Gradually add sugar, beating well after each addition. Spread onto cupcakes.

SPECIAL EXTRA

Add 1 tsp. lemon zest to frosting before spreading onto cupcakes. Garnish each cupcake with a small twist of lemon zest.

CHOCOLATE ELEGANCE

PREP: 20 min. \ **TOTAL:** 4 hours 35 min. \ **MAKES:** 14 servings

---

1½ pkg. (8 oz. each) *Philadelphia* Cream Cheese (12 oz.), softened

½ cup sugar

2½ cups thawed *Cool Whip* Whipped Topping, divided

6 oz. *Baker's* Semi-Sweet Chocolate, divided

1 pkg. (3.9 oz.) *Jell-O* Chocolate Instant Pudding

½ cup cold milk

¼ cup *Planters* Sliced Almonds, toasted

1 **Beat** cream cheese and sugar with mixer until well blended. Stir in 1½ cups *Cool Whip*; spread 2 cups onto bottom of 8×4-inch loaf pan lined with plastic wrap.

2 **Melt** 3 oz. chocolate. Add to remaining cream cheese mixture along with dry pudding mix and milk; beat 2 min. Spread over layer in pan. Refrigerate 4 hours.

3 **Microwave** remaining chocolate and *Cool Whip* in microwaveable bowl on HIGH 1 min.; stir until blended. Cool slightly.

4 **Invert** dessert onto platter. Remove pan and plastic wrap. Spread dessert with glaze; top with nuts. Refrigerate until glaze is firm.

SIMPLY SENSATIONAL TRUFFLES

PREP: 20 min. \ **TOTAL:** 2 hours 20 min. \ **MAKES:** 3 doz. or 18 servings, 2 truffles each

---

20 oz. *Baker's* **Semi-Sweet Chocolate, divided**

1 pkg. (8 oz.) *Philadelphia* **Cream Cheese, softened**

Decorations: chopped *Planters* **Cocktail Peanuts, multi-colored sprinkles**

1 **Melt** 8 oz. chocolate as directed on package. Beat cream cheese in medium bowl with mixer until creamy. Blend in melted chocolate. Refrigerate 1 hour or until firm.

2 **Cover** baking sheet with waxed paper. Shape chocolate mixture into 36 balls, using about 2 tsp. for each. Place in single layer on prepared baking sheet.

3 **Melt** remaining chocolate. Use fork to dip truffles in chocolate; return to baking sheet. Decorate, then refrigerate 1 hour.

CREAMY LEMON NUT BARS

PREP: 15 min. \ **TOTAL:** 1 hour \ **MAKES:** 32 servings

- ½ **cup butter, softened**
- ⅓ **cup powdered sugar**
- 2 **tsp. vanilla**
- 1¾ **cups flour, divided**
- ⅓ **cup chopped *Planters* Pecans**
- 1 **pkg. (8 oz.) *Philadelphia* Cream Cheese, softened**
- 2 **cups granulated sugar**
- 3 **eggs**
- 1 **Tbsp. lemon zest**
- ½ **cup lemon juice**
- 1 **Tbsp. powdered sugar**

1 **Heat** oven to 350°F.

2 **Line** 13×9-inch baking pan with foil; spray with cooking spray. Mix butter, ⅓ cup powdered sugar and vanilla in large bowl. Gradually stir in 1½ cups flour and pecans. Press dough firmly onto bottom of prepared pan. Bake 15 min.

3 **Beat** cream cheese and granulated sugar in medium bowl with electric mixer on high speed until well blended. Add remaining ¼ cup flour and eggs; beat until blended. Stir in lemon zest and juice. Pour over crust.

4 **Bake** 30 min. or until center is set. Cool completely. Sprinkle with 1 Tbsp. powdered sugar just before serving.

SUBSTITUTE

Prepare as directed, using lime zest and lime juice.

TIRAMISU BOWL

PREP: 20 min. \ **TOTAL:** 2 hours 20 min. \ **MAKES:** 16 servings, about ⅔ cup each

---

 1 pkg. (8 oz.) *Philadelphia* Cream Cheese, softened

 2 pkg. (3.4 oz. each) *Jell-O* Vanilla Flavor Instant Pudding

 3 cups cold milk

 1 tub (8 oz.) *Cool Whip* Whipped Topping, thawed, divided

48 vanilla wafers

 ½ cup brewed strong *Maxwell House* Coffee, cooled, divided

 2 oz. *Baker's* Semi-Sweet Chocolate, grated

 1 cup fresh raspberries

1 **Beat** cream cheese with mixer until creamy. Add dry pudding mixes and milk; beat 2 min. Gently stir in *Cool Whip*.

2 **Line** 2½-qt. bowl with 24 wafers; drizzle with ¼ cup coffee. Top with half each of the pudding mixture and chocolate. Repeat all layers.

3 **Top** with remaining *Cool Whip* and raspberries. Refrigerate 2 hours.

HOW TO EASILY GRATE CHOCOLATE

Before grating the chocolate, microwave it on HIGH for 10 sec. or just until slightly softened.

RED VELVET CUPCAKES

PREP: 15 min. \ **TOTAL:** 1 hour 15 min. \ **MAKES:** 24 servings

---

- **1 pkg. (2-layer size) red velvet cake mix**
- **1 pkg. (3.9 oz.) *Jell-O* Chocolate Instant Pudding**
- **1 pkg. (8 oz.) *Philadelphia* Cream Cheese, softened**
- **½ cup butter or margarine, softened**
- **1 pkg. (16 oz.) powdered sugar (about 4 cups)**
- **1 cup thawed *Cool Whip* Whipped Topping**
- **1 oz. *Baker's* White Chocolate, shaved into curls**

1 Prepare cake batter and bake as directed on package for 24 cupcakes, blending dry pudding mix into batter before spooning into prepared muffin cups. Cool.

2 Beat cream cheese and butter in large bowl with mixer until well blended. Gradually beat in sugar. Whisk in *Cool Whip*. Spoon 1½ cups into small freezer-weight resealable plastic bag; seal bag. Cut small corner off bottom of bag. Insert tip of bag into top of each cupcake to pipe about 1 Tbsp. frosting into center of cupcake.

3 Frost cupcakes with remaining frosting; top with chocolate curls. Keep refrigerated.